DANGEROUS DINOSAURS
KILLER DINOSAURS

Liz Miles

W
FRANKLIN WATTS
LONDON•SYDNEY

First published in 2015 by Franklin Watts

Copyright © Arcturus Holdings Limited

Franklin Watts
338 Euston Road
London
NW1 3BH

Franklin Watts Australia
Level 17/207 Kent Street, Sydney, NSW 2000

Produced by Arcturus Publishing Limited,
26/27 Bickels Yard, 151–153 Bermondsey Street, London SE1 3HA

Author: Liz Miles
Editors: Joe Harris, Alex Woolf and Joe Fullman
Designer: Emma Randall
Original design concept: Notion Design

Picture Credits:
Key: b-bottom, m-middle, l-left, r-right, t-top
All images by pixel-shack.com except for:
Arcturus Image Library: p13 t.
Corbis: p24 b.
Shutterstock: p25 t, p25 b.
Wikipedia Commons: p6 b, p23 b.

A CIP catalogue record for this book is available from the British Library.

Dewey Decimal Classification Number: 567.9'12-dc23
ISBN: 978 1 4451 4156 5

Printed in China

Franklin Watts is a division of Hachette Children's Books, an Hachette
UK company.
www.hachette.co.uk

SL004435UK

Supplier 03, Date 1214, Print Run 3761

CONTENTS

ULTIMATE PREDATORS

Killer dinosaurs – the meat-eaters – were among the deadliest animals ever to roam this planet. They took many forms, ranging from giant theropods with bone-crushing jaws and flesh-ripping teeth, to small but fleet-footed raptors with grasping hands and slashing claws.

These carnivores used many different methods to catch and kill their prey. Some hunted alone, while others worked in packs. Some had powerful toothless beaks, while others had needle-sharp teeth. Some used speed, while others relied on enormous muscle power, deadly kicks or super-sized bites.

Seen here hunting by a waterhole, the terrifying T. rex was one of the top predators of its day.

SMART AND DEADLY

Meat-eating dinosaurs, such as Allosaurus (al-loh-SORE-us) had good eyesight, a keen sense of smell and a large brain to plan hunting strategies. They also had long, strong legs to run fast and catch their prey. The biggest carnivorous dinosaur was Spinosaurus (SPINE-oh-SORE-us), at about 18 m (59 ft) long. The smallest was probably Hesperonychus (HES-pare-RON-i-kus) at just 1 m (3.3 ft).

TYRANT LIZARD

Tyrannosaurus rex (tie-RAN-oh-SORE-us REX) means 'tyrant lizard'. This terrifying creature was one of the strongest and biggest of the dinosaur predators, stalking the land in the last part of the Cretaceous period. It grew to 12 m (39 ft) in length and its jaws alone were 1.4 m (4.5 ft) long and filled with ferocious teeth the size of large daggers.

Because of its oddly weak little arms, some scientists think that T. rex fed on carrion rather than living prey. But others say that it would have needed more than carcasses to satisfy its hunger and that its forward-facing eyes were designed to spot and judge the distance of fast-moving prey.

POWER MUSCLES

Bulky muscles gave this monster incredible power and legs strong enough to carry its massive body weight of 4,500 kg (5 tons). Like an elephant, it could probably walk fast, but its weight would have made running difficult.

DINOSAUR DETECTIVES

Fossils of Tyrannosaurus rex jaws show how it had a very wide bite. There was an extra jaw joint, so that, like a snake, T. rex could almost dislocate its jaws. This would have allowed its mouth to open extraordinarily wide. The strength and thickness of the skull bones suggest it had powerful jaw muscles, strong enough to crush bones.

RAZOR TEETH
The pointed front teeth were designed for grabbing and puncturing thick skin, while the back teeth were blade shaped for sawing through bones, flesh and muscle.

LETHAL BITE
A T. rex bite mark on the fossil of a duckbill was used to work out the power of its bite. Scientists estimate a bite force of 1,365 kg (1.5 tons), more than three times that of an African lion. Rather than battle with its prey, the T. rex's aim would have been to cripple it with one chomp. Once its prey had fallen, the bone-crushing jaws could then finish it off.

LITTLE ARMS
Although a hunter, Tyrannosaurus rex had small, weak arms and two-fingered hands that would not have even reached its mouth! Perhaps these arms were used to steady its vast body as it stood up.

RAVENOUS GIANT

Giganotosaurus (jig-an-OH-toe-SORE-us) was definitely gigantic – this beast was as heavy as a truck and, at 13 m (46 ft), it was longer than a T. rex. This killer dinosaur lived alongside – and probably hunted – giant plant-eating titanosaurs, on the South American plains.

DEADLY DINO DISCOVERY

For a hundred years Tyrannosaurus rex was the biggest land predator known, but in 1993 an even bigger one was discovered. Named Giganotosaurus, it has the longest theropod jaws ever found, measuring 1.8 m (5.9 ft) – longer than many adult humans are tall! It lived around 30 million years before T. rex and had three fingers on each hand – better for gripping than T. rex's two. Its bite was less powerful, but its blade-like cutting teeth could easily slice through skin and bone.

KILLER PAIRS

Giganotosaurus wasn't afraid to hunt creatures much bigger than itself and was probably the only predator of Argentinosaurus (AR-gen-tee-no-SORE-us), which was three times taller. Scientists believe that Giganotosaurus may have hunted in pairs or groups of six or more, using its powerful jaws to bite at the legs of the slow-moving sauropods until they weakened from bleeding and fell down. The Giganotosaurus pack would then move in to tear at the meat and consume the carcass.

VITAL STATISTICS

GIGANOTOSAURUS

Meaning of name: Giant southern lizard

Family: Allosauridae

Period: Late Cretaceous

Size: 7 m / 23 ft height; 13 m / 46 ft length

Weight: 7,300 kg / 8 tons

Diet: Meat

HUGE HUNGER

One sauropod kill could probably have satisfied a Giganotosaurus's hunger for a few weeks. There would have been no competition from other meat-eating hunters because of Giganotosaurus's size and power. The giant predators may have been surprisingly fast too. Scientists estimate they could have attained speeds of up to 50 km/h (31 mph).

UTAHRAPTOR

VICIOUS PACK HUNTER

Utahraptor (YOO-ta-RAP-tor) was an intelligent, agile and swift hunter. It had a stiff tail to help it stay balanced as it pounced on its prey. As heavy as a large bear, it was the biggest of the dromaeosaurids or 'running lizards' (also called raptors).

QUITE A BITE

The Utahraptor's powerful jaws were crammed with razor-sharp teeth, which it used to bite and grasp its prey once it had pulled it down with its claws.

WHO YOU CALLIN' CHICKEN?

Fossils show a bone structure similar to a chicken's, and scientists believe it also had feathers. However, in spite of the feathers it couldn't fly, and any feathery covering would have been for warmth, or for show to attract a mate.

KILLER CLAWS

Utahraptor's sickle-shaped claws were its prize weapons. It raised these off the ground as it ran. The 35 cm (14 in) long blades could tear at its prey or cling on like climbing crampons. With a powerful kick, the claw could have brought down another dinosaur, often killing it instantly.

Like wolves, Utahraptors stalked their prey in packs. Working together, they could have brought down even large sauropods. They would cling to their prey's bodies, biting and tearing until their victims were exhausted.

UTAHRAPTOR VERSUS WOLF

How do these pack hunters measure up?

	UTAHRAPTOR	WOLF
HEIGHT	3 m / 9.9 ft	0.85 m / 2.83 ft
WEIGHT	1,000 kg / 1.1 tons	60 kg / 130 lb
SPEED	30 kph / 20 mph	60 kph / 37 mph
BITE FORCE	460 kg / 1014 lbs	66 kg / 145 lbs
EYESIGHT	Excellent	Very good

SICKLE-CLAWED RUNNERS

Utahraptor belonged to a family of dinosaurs called dromaeosaurids (DROM-ee-oh-SORE-ids). Speed, agility, good eyesight and – above all – sharp weapons made them one of the deadliest groups of predators. Although their bodies look bird-like, they had powerful legs for running at high speeds and stiff tails to help with balance as they kicked and slashed with their sickle-shaped toe claws.

FEARSOME TALONS

As part of a group called maniraptora ('hand-grabbers'), dromaeosaurids had strong, grasping hands, often with fearsome finger talons. Scientists believe that, relative to their body weight, dromaeosaurids had the biggest brains of all the dinosaurs, and so were among the most intelligent.

'TERRIBLE CLAW'

Deinonychus (die-NON-ee-KUS) means 'terrible claw' and its sickle claw was as sharp as a meat cleaver. Its eyes could look forward, giving binocular vision, so it could assess the distance of prey more accurately and judge the point at which it was close enough to kick, grab or leap for an accurate attack. Its curved sawing teeth bit and tore flesh from the bones of its prey. A study of Deinonychus led scientists to believe it was probably warm-blooded, so its feather covering was necessary to maintain its temperature – unlike cold-blooded creatures, which did not need the insulation.

Dromaeosaurids like Velociraptor (vel-OSS-ee-rap-tor) had four toes, but fossil tracks show only two-toed footprints. Its first toe was a dewclaw, a small toe on its leg which did not touch the ground. The second toe, with its large claw, was held above the ground. It walked on its third and fourth toes.

HACK ATTACK

The use of the sickle-shaped claw as a deadly weapon has been proven by a fossil find. A Velociraptor's second toe claw was found attached to the ribs of a Protoceratops (pro-toe-SER-ah-tops). The sheep-sized plant-eater was clearly trying to fight off the Velociraptor when both died suddenly in mid-battle, perhaps in a landslide.

TIPTOE

Velociraptor raised its second toe when it walked so the claw did not touch the ground. This was to prevent it from becoming blunt. When Velociraptor attacked, it used its powerful kick to stab the razor-sharp claw into its prey.

CARNOTAURUS

'FLESH-EATING BULL'

Carnotaurus (KAR-no-TORE-us) means 'flesh-eating bull'. With two horns and a powerful, bulky body, this theropod certainly had a bull-like appearance. It had a hunter's forward-facing vision and legs that could chase prey at high speed. Less powerful were its puzzlingly small arms, each with four fingers. It also had weak teeth and jaw muscles.

Carnotaurus didn't have a powerful bite (only 340 kg / 0.3 tons – much weaker than T. rex's 1,360 kg / 1.5 tons). However, it had the muscles to head-butt its prey. Its unusual skull was made up of separate moving parts, so it could absorb more pressure during head butts or bites.

SCENT OF FRESH MEAT

Carnotaurus probably followed its nose to find its prey. Its deep skull had an especially large hole in front of the eye sockets, suggesting that the dinosaur's sense of smell was above average for a hunter. It probably stalked its prey by following its scent.

HORN FIGHTER

Carnotaurus's horns stick out sideways just above the eyes, and may have been used in male-to-male fights. They may also have been used to help knock out its prey, or for display in the mating season. Its strong neck would have given Carnotaurus colossal power if it butted a rival. For extra protection in sparring or attacks, Carnotaurus had pebbly, lizard-like skin with larger lumps down its back.

VITAL STATISTICS

CARNOTAURUS

Meaning of name:
Flesh-eating bull

Family: Abelisauridae

Period: Mid Cretaceous

Size: 3 m / 9.8 ft height;
7.5 m / 25 ft length

Weight: 1,000 kg / 1.1 tons

Diet: Meat

TROODON

NIGHT TRACKER

Troodon (TROH-oh-don) had a body that was similar in shape to an ostrich, yet unlike any ostrich living today, it was a killer. This meat-eater is estimated to have had more than 100 teeth, all sharp and triangular with serrated edges for cutting.

Troodon teeth have been found near fossils of baby hadrosaurs, suggesting they enjoyed tucking into vulnerable hatchlings. Troodon means 'wounding tooth'. The creature was named after a single pointed tooth from an early discovery.

QUICK THINKER

Troodon had an unusually large brain compared to its body weight, making it one of the more intelligent dinosaurs.

KILLER TOES

Long legs meant a long stride, so Troodon could probably run fast. At the end of each second toe there was a curved claw, which could have done serious damage to any creature it was chasing.

GRABBING CLAWS

Troodon's clawed hands could meet palm to palm, so they could get a firm grasp on small living prey.

NIGHT VISION

Large, forward-facing eyes gave Troodon binocular vision and may also have enabled it to hunt in poor light, such as at dusk, or even at night like a cat. A pack of troodon would have been capable of bringing down prey much larger than themselves.

TROODON VERSUS CAT

How do these night hunters measure up?

	TROODON	DOMESTIC CAT
HEIGHT	1 m / 40 in	0.20-0.25 m / 8-10 in
WEIGHT	45 kg / 99 lb	3-4 kg / 7-9 lb
SPEED	40 kph / 25 mph	48 kph / 30 mph
NUMBER OF TEETH	100+	30
EYESIGHT	Excellent	Excellent

TERRIFYING TEETH

Dinosaur teeth were harder than bone, and so were more often preserved as fossils. Scientists can work out a great deal from fossilised teeth, such as what the dinosaurs ate.

MASSIVE EATER

Allosaurus, a 3-tonne (3.3 ton) predator that lived in Jurassic times, had teeth with serrated edges for sawing through flesh. The teeth were 5–10 cm (2–4 in) long and relatively small for a predator, but they were pointed and curved backwards – perfect for tearing off giant chunks of its victims' flesh. Allosaurus bite marks have been found in the backbone of an Apatosaurus (a-PAT-oh-SORE-us), a huge sauropod, and the neck bone of the plated Stegosaurus (STE-go-SORE-us) – proof of the deadliness of its teeth. If any teeth broke off or were worn down, they were shed, and new teeth grew in their place, so the Allosaurus was never without its lethal bite.

FLESH SAWS

Some scientists believe that predators like Allosaurus would have used their teeth like a rasp, to strip off flesh from still-living prey. Rather than attacking it head-on and risking injury, they would instead wait for their victim to slowly bleed to death.

TYPES OF TEETH

We can identify plant-eaters from their peg-like teeth or sharp but toothless beaks, which were used for grazing. The meat- and fish-eaters had terrifying teeth – strong and sharp for grabbing and catching their prey, for tearing at flesh and crushing bone.

VENOMOUS BITE

Some scientists have suggested that Sinornithosaurus (SINE-or-nith-oh-SORE-us) used its curved, snake-like fangs to inject venom into its prey. This feathered, bird-like dinosaur, though no bigger than a turkey, may have killed prey much bigger than itself, by first subduing it with its venomous bite.

 # DINOSAUR DETECTIVES

We can discover how powerful a dinosaur's bite was from the size and shape of its tooth fossils, and from making reconstructions of its jaws to shows its muscles and their likely power. Tooth marks in a victim's fossils may be useful clues to bite strength, but they do not prove that the biter killed its victim. The victim may have already been dead and the meat-eater could have been feeding on its carcass.

BARYONYX

FISH HUNTER

Although slightly smaller than its famous relative, Spinosaurus, Baryonyx (bah-ree-ON-iks) was no less deadly. It is one of the few fish-hunting dinosaurs so far discovered, but had the lethal weapons necessary to ensure its success.

Some scientists suggest that although Baryonyx was a land animal, it swam in rivers and lakes too, hunting from the surface of the water. It may also have caught fish from the shoreline, like a crocodile. It was thought to have eaten only fish until the bones of an Iguanodon (ig-WHA-no-don) were found in the stomach of one of its fossils. So it probably took every opportunity to grab any kind of meaty meal.

VITAL STATISTICS

BARYONYX

Meaning of name: Heavy claw

Family: Spinosauridae

Period: Early Cretaceous

Size: 2.5 m / 8 ft height; 10 m / 33 ft length

Weight: 1,800 kg / 2 tons

Diet: Fish and meat

A FULL STOMACH

The fossilised remains of fish scales, fish bones and partially digested Iguanodon bones found in the stomach of a Baryonyx tell us about its diet.

CAGE OF TEETH

Its 96 long, pointed teeth were designed for capturing and gripping fish. A dip in its lower jaw may have helped to keep hold of any slippery, struggling fish too.

FISH SNATCHER

Baryonyx had long crocodile-like jaws that it could dip into the water to snatch fish. Like a crocodile, it may have used the tip of its jaws to sense any movement in the water and so be able to open its mouth just in time to catch any passing prey.

HUGE CLAW

Baryonyx's name means 'heavy claw' and refers to the 0.3 m (1 ft) long claws on its thumbs. It may have used these like skewers or knives, to stab and tear the fish that it had caught, making it ready to eat. Its teeth were too spiked to do the job – designed to catch, not crush or chew.

PACKS AND FAMILIES

Predators did not always hunt or live alone. Some, such as Velociraptor, may have roamed around and hunted in packs.

STRENGTH IN NUMBERS

Protoceratops (shown below) would have lived in large herds for protection. However, if a young, sick or old animal became separated from the others, it could become a target for predators, such as these Velociraptors. The Protoceratops' horns and frill could perhaps have fended off a single attacker, but against a group it would have stood little chance.

TEAMWORK

Working together, a pack of Velociraptors would have made short work of a lone Protoceratops. Like a modern pride of lions, the predators would have cooperated to bring down their prey. One would have attacked the horned head, while another went for the unguarded rear of the creature.

FAMILY PROTECTION

Even the most powerful dinosaurs, such as Allosaurus (shown here) were vulnerable to predators when young. Allosaurus nested in groups, probably for shared protection. In one Allosaurus nesting site, scientists found fossil bones of different aged creatures, from hatchlings to elderly adults. There were no young adults, however, so perhaps they were thought strong enough to go off and fend for themselves. Fossil bones of hadrosaurs with Allosaurus bite marks were also found there, indicating they were the families' source of food.

DINOSAUR DETECTIVES

We know that a carnivorous dinosaur called Albertosaurus (al-BERT-oh-SORE-us) moved around in packs because the fossil bones of 26 Albertosauruses were discovered in one area of Canada. The dinosaurs were of all different ages, from 2 to 23. Forty Allosaurus were also found in one area of Utah, USA. They may have died while trapped in mud – along with the dinosaurs they were hunting.

SAVAGE KILLERS

OR JUST SCAVENGERS?

Not all meat-eating dinosaurs would have killed their own prey. Many carnivores were actually scavengers – tearing the flesh from corpses of dinosaurs. Bite marks on fossilised bones and scavenger teeth trapped in dinosaur skeletons are evidence of this. They show that some dinosaurs lived off the skeletons left behind after hunters had eaten their fill.

DID T. REX HUNT?

Some scientists think that Tyrannosaurus rex may have been a scavenger and not a killer at all. They argue that its good sense of smell and small arms seem better suited to a carcass-eater than a killer. It would have sniffed out faraway carrion and eaten the dead bodies of creatures killed by other predators, or dead from other causes.

THE TRUTH ABOUT T. REX

No one has yet been able to prove that Tyrannosaurus rex was definitely a hunter, or definitely a scavenger. There is not yet enough evidence. However, many scientists suspect that both are true. They argue that T. rex, like many large predators living today, would have been an opportunist. It would have eaten live prey when it could, but would not have turned up its nose at carcasses.

BULLY TACTICS

A modern animal that both hunts and scavenges is the hyena. Hyenas are known for driving away lions to steal their kill. It's likely that many dinosaurs would have done the same. T. rex would have been especially effective at driving smaller hunters away from their meals. Smaller scavengers probably picked at the remains after a bigger killer ate its fill.

DINOSAUR DETECTIVES

Fossilised fragments of Velociraptor teeth have been found close to the scarred fossil bones of Protoceratops. This suggests that this small carnivore regularly scavenged carcasses, as well as catching fresh meat when it was available.

DINO WORLD

Killer dinosaur fossils have been discovered on every continent of the world. The map shows a few examples.

ALBERTOSAURUS

FOUND IN: North America
WHEN IT LIVED:
Late Cretaceous
(76-74 million years ago)
The first Albertosaurus fossil found (in 1884) was a skull, sticking out of the soil near the Red Deer River in Alberta, Canada. Since then at least 30 been found, including 22 near the river – showing that they travelled in packs.

UTAHRAPTOR

FOUND IN: North America
WHEN IT LIVED: Early
Cretaceous (112-100 million years ago)
Only fragments of Utahraptor have been found – but enough to work out its size and other features. They were found in the Arches National Park, Utah, which would have been wooded in Utahraptor's time.

TROODON

FOUND IN: North America
WHEN IT LIVED: Late Cretaceous
(74-65 million years ago)
Fossil pieces from different types of Troodon have been found all around North America, including in Alberta, Canada and Wyoming and Montana, USA.

CARNOTAURUS

FOUND IN: South America
WHEN IT LIVED: Late Cretaceous
(70 million years ago)
A near-complete fossilised Carnotaurus skeleton, along with impressions of its bumpy skin, has been found in the Chubut Province of Argentina.

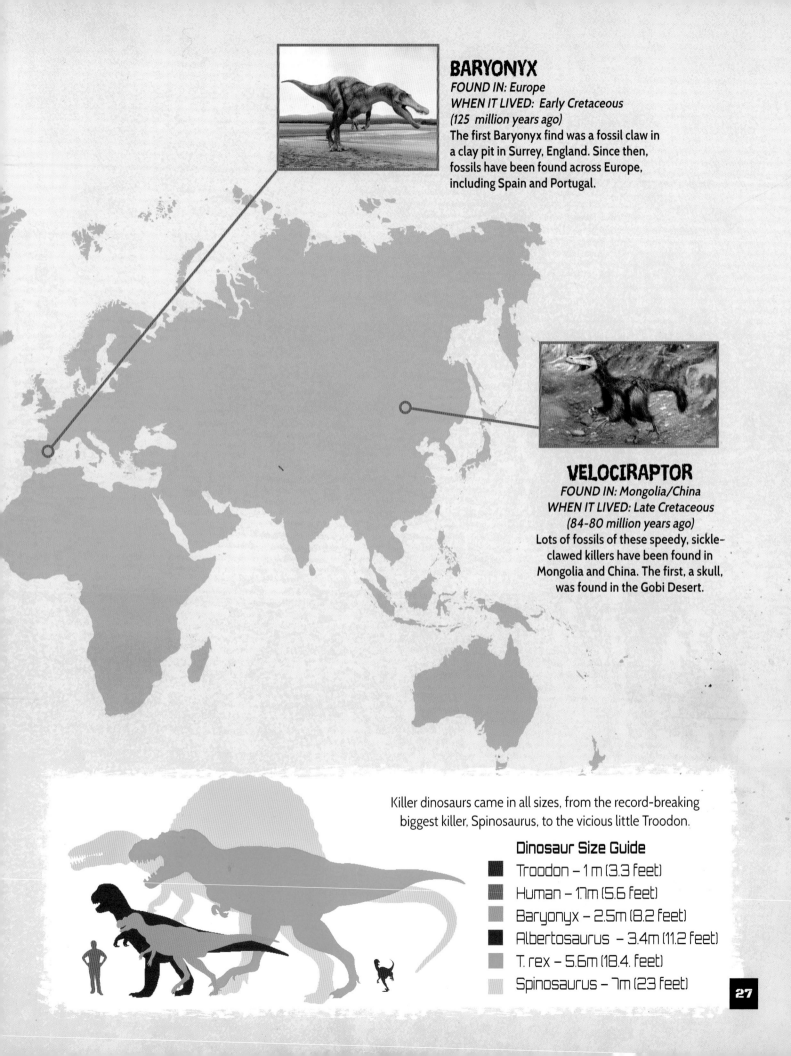

BARYONYX
FOUND IN: Europe
WHEN IT LIVED: Early Cretaceous
(125 million years ago)
The first Baryonyx find was a fossil claw in a clay pit in Surrey, England. Since then, fossils have been found across Europe, including Spain and Portugal.

VELOCIRAPTOR
FOUND IN: Mongolia/China
WHEN IT LIVED: Late Cretaceous
(84-80 million years ago)
Lots of fossils of these speedy, sickle-clawed killers have been found in Mongolia and China. The first, a skull, was found in the Gobi Desert.

Killer dinosaurs came in all sizes, from the record-breaking biggest killer, Spinosaurus, to the vicious little Troodon.

Dinosaur Size Guide
- Troodon – 1 m (3.3 feet)
- Human – 1.7m (5.6 feet)
- Baryonyx – 2.5m (8.2 feet)
- Albertosaurus – 3.4m (11.2 feet)
- T. rex – 5.6m (18.4. feet)
- Spinosaurus – 7m (23 feet)

TIMELINE

OF LIFE ON EARTH

Scientists have divided the billions of years of prehistoric time into periods. Dinosaurs lived in the Triassic, Cretaceous and Jurassic periods, while modern humans evolved in the Quaternary period.

← CAMBRIAN
541–485 mya:
Life forms become
more complex.

↓ SILURIAN
443–419 mya:
First creatures on land.

↑ ORDOVICIAN
485–443 mya:
Arthropods (creatures with exoskeletons) rule the seas. Plants colonise the land.

↑ PRECAMBRIAN
4,570–541 million years ago (mya): The first life forms appear. They are tiny, one-celled creatures.

↑ DEVONIAN
419–359 mya: First insects evolve.
Fish now dominate the seas.

↓ CRETACEOUS

145–65 mya: Spinosaurus and T. rex evolve. Dinosaur extinction.

↘ QUATERNARY

2.6 mya– today: Woolly mammoths roam the Earth, modern humans evolve.

← PALEOGENE/ NEOGENE

65–2.6 mya: Many giant mammal species emerge

↓ TRIASSIC

252–201 mya: First dinosaurs.

↑ JURASSIC

201–145 mya: The largest dinosaurs evolve.

↑ TODAY

← PERMIAN

299–252 mya: First therapsids (ancestors of mammals) evolve.

← CARBONIFEROUS

359–299 mya: Reptiles first appear, vast forests cover the land.

GLOSSARY

Carboniferous A prehistoric period when there were many swamps and forests. Fossil fuels later formed from the trees and plants that died.

carcass The body of a dead creature.

carrion Flesh from a creature that has died, and a source of food for some birds and animals.

Cretaceous A prehistoric period during which mammals and giant dinosaurs lived, and which ended with the mass extinction of the dinosaurs 65 million years ago.

Devonian A prehistoric period, also known as the Age of Fishes, when the oceans were warm and filled with many types of evolving fish.

evolve To change gradually over time.

fossil The remains of a prehistoric organism preserved in rock.

fossilised Made into a fossil.

frill A bony area around the neck of a dinosaur.

grazing Feeding on low-growing plants.

hadrosaurs Plant-eating family of dinosaurs, also known as duck-billed dinosaurs because of their beak-like mouths.

insulation A way of keeping heat in and cold out.

Jurassic A prehistoric period in which many large dinosaurs lived. It is also called the Age of Reptiles.

plates Bony sections on the surface of a dinosaur that gave it protection. Some plates stood up from the spine, as on a Stegosaurus.

predator An animal that hunts other animals to kill and eat.

prey An animal that is hunted by other animals for food.

reptiles Cold-blooded animals that usually lay eggs and have scales.

sauropods A group of giant, four-legged plant-eating dinosaurs with small heads, long necks and tails.

scavenger An animal that feeds on dead animals but does not kill them itself.

serrated Having a jagged, saw-like edge.

therapods A group of two-legged, mainly meat-eating dinosaurs, such as Tyrannosaurus rex and Giganotosaurus.

titanosaur A type of enormous sauropod from the Cretaceous period.

Triassic A prehistoric period during which the first dinosaurs and mammals evolved.

FURTHER READING

Dinosaur Record Breakers by Darren Naish (Carlton Kids, 2014)

Dinosaurs: A Children's Encyclopedia by editors of DK (Dorling Kindersley, 2011)

Evolution Revolution by Robert Winston (Dorling Kindersley, 2009)

National Geographic Kids: The Ultimate Dinopedia by Don Lessem
(National Geographic Society, 2012)

Prehistoric Safari: Giant Dinosaurs by Liz Miles (Franklin Watts, 2012)

The Usborne World Atlas of Dinosaurs by Susanna Davidson
(Usborne Publishing, 2013)

WEBSITES

http://www.bbc.co.uk/nature/14343366
A regularly updated part of the BBC website, dedicated to dinosaurs.
There is a news section and plenty of cool videos.

http://animals.nationalgeographic.com/animals/prehistoric/
This part of the National Geographic website is home to some fascinating articles
about dinosaurs. There are also some excellent pictures.

www.nhm.ac.uk/kids-only/index.html
The young people's section of the Natural History Museum website. Packed
with downloads, games, quizzes and lots of information about dinosaurs.

INDEX

SERIES CONTENTS

DINOSAUR DEFENDERS
Attack and Defence • Triceratops: Horn-Faced Fighter • Frightening Frills • Pachycephalosaurids: Butting Boneheads • Stegosaurus: Savage Spiker • Ankylosaurs: Defensive Demons • Hadrosaurs: Deafening Duckbills • Sauropods: Tail-Thrashing Titans • Patterns and Feathers • Herding Heavies • Danger Senses • Dino World • Timeline of Life on Earth

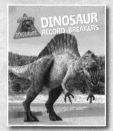

DINOSAUR RECORD-BREAKERS
Battling Giants • Titanosaurs: The Heavyweights • Smallest Dinosaurs • Ultimate Hunter: Spinosaurus • Deadliest Dinosaur • Skyscrapers • Dinosaur Egg Records • Fastest Dinosaurs • Longest Claws • Tough as Tanks: Best Protection • Smart Cookies or Bird Brains? • Famous Fossils • Timeline of Life on Earth

DINOSAURS AND THE PREHISTORIC WORLD
Dinosaur Planet • Changing Earth • Timeline of Life on Earth • Underwater Creatures • Emerging onto the Land • Early Reptiles: Fierce Forerunners • The First Dinosaurs: Hungry Hunters • Age of the Dinosaurs • Dino Diets • Extinction Event • After the Dinosaurs: Savage Mammals • Descendants of the Dinosaurs • Dino World

KILLER DINOSAURS
Ultimate Predators • Tyrant Lizard • Ravenous Giant • Utahraptor: Vicious Pack Hunter • Sickle-Clawed Runners • Carnotaurus: 'Flesh-Eating Bull' • Troodon: Night Tracker • Terrifying Teeth • Baryonyx: Fish Hunter • Packs and Families • Savage Killers or Just Scavengers? • Dino World • Timeline of Life on Earth

FLYING MONSTERS
Savage Skies • Needle-Toothed Terrors • Pteranodons: Awesome Axe-Heads • Jutting-Jawed Pterosaurs • Dimorphodon: Tooth-Beaked Hunter • Furry Fiends • Quetzalcoatlus: Giant Vulture • Crested Competitors • Keen Eyed Killers • Bird-Like Biters • Flying Families • Winged World • Timeline of Life on Earth

SEA MONSTERS
From the Deep • Shell Shock • Cameroceras: Tentacled Terror • Super-Sharks • Long-Necked Hunters • Liopleurodon: Jurassic Tyrant • Massive-Jawed Monsters • Ichthyosaurs: Fish-Lizards • Fearsome Fish • Giant Crocs • Changing Seas • Fossil Finds • Timeline of Life on Earth